Eucharist

A Catechesis for Middle Grades

General Editor
Rev. Gerard P. Weber, S.T.L.

Contributing Editors
Irene H. Murphy
Helen P. Whitaker

Benziger Publishing Company
Mission Hills, California

Illustrations:
Kevin Davidson, Rosanne Litzinger, Mike Muir, Linda Sullivan, Susan Staroba, Maryann Thomas

Photography:
Richard Hutchings, Stephen McBrady, Alan Oddi/Photo Edit, James Shaffer

Nihil Obstat:
Msgr. Joseph Pollard, S.T.D., V.F.
Censor Deputatus

Imprimatur:
†Roger M. Mahony
Cardinal of Los Angeles
December 6, 1994

The nihil obstat and imprimatur are official declarations that a book or pamphlet is free of doctrinal or moral error. No implication is contained therein that those who have granted the nihil obstat and imprimatur agree with the contents, opinions, or statements expressed.

Scripture passages are taken from the *New American Bible with Revised New Testament*. Revised New Testament of the New American Bible, copyright © 1986 by the Confraternity of Christian Doctrine, Washington, D.C. All rights reserved. Old Testament of the New American Bible, copyright © 1970 by the Confraternity of Christian Doctrine. All rights reserved.

Copyright © 1996 by Glencoe/McGraw-Hill. All rights reserved. Except as permitted under the United States Copyright Act, no part of this publication may be reproduced or distributed in any form or by any means, or stored in a database or retrieval system, without prior written permission from the publisher.

Send all inquiries to:
BENZIGER PUBLISHING COMPANY
15319 Chatsworth Street
Mission Hills, California 91345

Printed in the United States of America.

ISBN 0-02-655934-X

1 2 3 4 5   WEB   99 98 97 96 95

Contents

1	Gathered Together	5
2	We Ask Forgiveness	13
3	Meeting Jesus in God's Word	21
4	All That We Have	29
5	Remember and Give Thanks	37
6	Give Us This Day	45
7	The Bread of Life	53
8	Love One Another	61

Glossary	69
Receiving Holy Communion	73
Important Things to Know	73
Parts of the Mass	75
Music	77
Prayers	79
Lists Catholics Remember	80

INTRODUCTION: WE CELEBRATE

1 Gathered Together

The Greeting

Priest: In the name of the Father, and of the Son, and of the Holy Spirit.

People: Amen.

Priest: The Lord be with you.

People: And also with you.

Introduction: We Celebrate

Belonging

Monica stood outside the door to the gymnasium. She could hear the bounce of a basketball and the cheers of a crowd. Everything sounded very exciting.

But Monica did not go in. This gymnasium belonged to a club, and only its members could get in. From what Monica had heard, the club only accepted people who could pass the entrance test.

Monica had studied hard for the test, but she was still afraid.

Suddenly, the gym door swung open. A sweaty girl wearing shorts and the club T-shirt ran out. She almost bumped into Monica.

"Sorry," the girl said as she ran to the water fountain and got a drink.

Monica watched the girl gulp down some water and then wipe her face on her shirt sleeve.

Join In!

"You're wearing high tops!" the girl exclaimed loudly. "I've been begging my parents for months now to get me a pair like that," the girl continued. "Do you play basketball? We could use a sub."

Monica relaxed a little and smiled. "Yes, I play," she admitted, "but I'm not a club member."

"Well, do you want to become one?"

"Sure."

"Do you know the rules?"

"By heart," Monica answered.

"And the club motto?"

"One family forever."

"What about the symbol on my T-shirt?"

INTRODUCTION: WE CELEBRATE

"The eagle stands for courage, and the dove stands for love."

"Good! Now you only need one more thing," the girl said. "Someone already in the club has to sponsor you as a new member."

Monica looked startled. "But I don't have a sponsor," she said with dismay.

"You do now," the girl stated. "I'm Toni, the team captain. If I say you're in our club, then you're in."

Monica stood there, too surprised to say anything.

Toni opened the gym door and waited. "Well, are you coming in or not?"

"But what about the entrance test?"

"You just passed it," Toni said with a laugh. "Welcome to the club!"

Thinking about the Story

- Why did Monica want to join the club?
- What did Toni do to help Monica?
- What does the story have to do with "belonging"?

Catholic Membership

When you were born, you became the newest member of your family. Your parents, brothers, and sisters accepted you and loved you. They protected you and helped you grow. They taught you certain rules. They let you know that you belong.

When your life began, you also became a new member of God's Family. When you were baptized, you became a member of a special part of God's Family—the Catholic Church. This Church has many members, all over the world. Some are old; some are young. Some are rich; some are poor. Everyone is welcome in the Catholic Church. Everyone can belong.

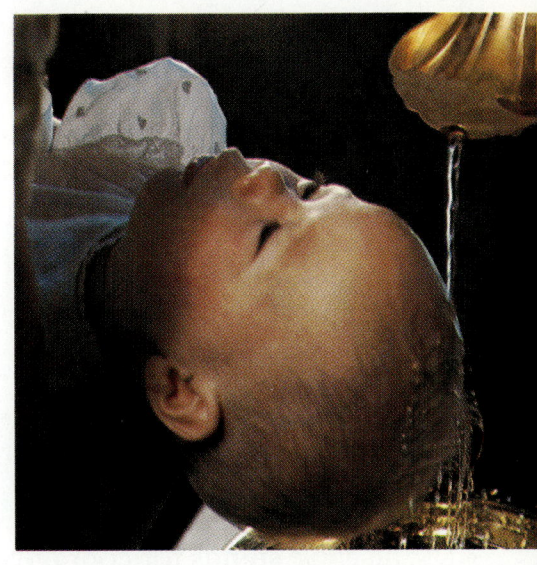

Baptism

Baptism is the "door" or "gate" into the Church. At baptism, the priest or deacon pours water over the new member's head. The water is a sign that the new member wants to wash away the past. It is a sign that the new member wants to start living as a follower of God's Son, Jesus. As the priest or deacon pours the water, he says, "I baptize you in the name of the Father, and of the Son, and of the Holy Spirit."

These same words are used at the beginning of Mass. They remind Catholics of their baptism. By this Sign of the Cross, Catholics say that they are members of God's Family, and they believe in the **Blessed Trinity**.

Signs of Belonging

Catholics have many ways to show that they belong to God's Family. First of all, they celebrate Mass every Sunday and on **holy days.** The members of God's Family come together at Mass to praise God. They give thanks for the wonderful gifts God has given to them. They remember all the ways God has loved them. They learn how to live more like Jesus.

DEVELOPMENT: WE BELIEVE

A second way Catholics show their membership is by receiving the **sacraments,** particularly the **Eucharist,** or Holy Communion. Catholics believe that the bread and wine offered at Mass truly become the Body and Blood of Jesus. Members of God's Family try to receive Communion often.

A third way Catholics show that they belong to God's Family is in their daily actions. Members of God's Family try to be faithful to the teachings of Jesus. They try to show love for one another. They try to choose what is right. They help others who are in need.

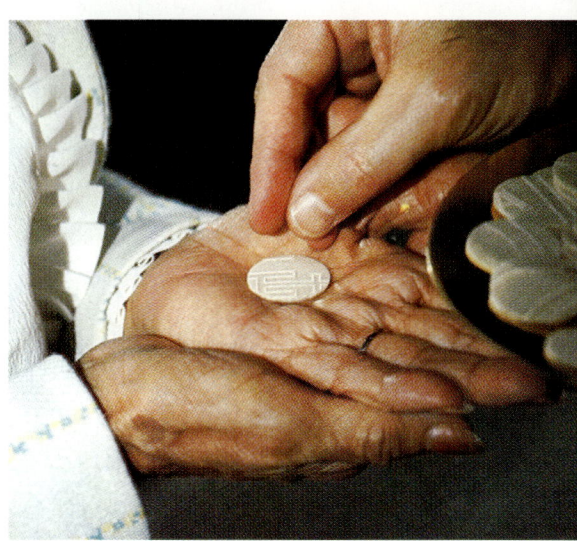

We Catholics Believe

The Catholic Church in the United States celebrates six **holy days:** The Solemnity of Mary, Mother of God (January 1); Ascension Thursday (forty days after Easter); The Assumption of Mary (August 15); All Saints' Day (November 1); The Immaculate Conception of Mary (December 8); and Christmas (December 25). Catholics show their membership in God's Family by celebrating Mass on these days.

Blessed Trinity is our name for the one God who is Father, Son, and Holy Spirit.

A **sacrament** is a special sign of God's life, or **grace,** and love. There are seven sacraments: Baptism, Confirmation, Eucharist, Reconciliation, Anointing of the Sick, Marriage, and Holy Orders.

Baptism is a sacrament that gives new life, washes away sin, and joins us to the Christian community.

Eucharist is the sacrament of Jesus' presence in Holy Commmunion at Mass.

9

Development: We Believe

The Good Shepherd

In the days of Jesus, many people raised sheep. Each night, they gathered their sheep and put them into pens. Often, there was a gatekeeper to watch over the gate to the pen. The gatekeeper made sure no robbers or wolves climbed over the fence or got through the gate. In the morning, only the shepherd of the sheep was allowed into the pen. He would speak to the sheep and they would recognize his voice. They would follow him out into the fields to eat and drink.

One day, Jesus spoke to the people. "I am the Good Shepherd," He said. "I know My sheep, and they know Me. I am not like a hired man, who is not a shepherd. Such a person does not care for the sheep. When he sees a wolf coming, he leaves the sheep and runs away. The wolf can then chase the sheep and scatter them."

"I am not like that," Jesus continued. "I care about My sheep. If a wolf came, I would stay and protect them. If a robber came, I would give up My life for My sheep. If one of them got lost, I would go and look for that sheep."

Another time, Jesus told the people, "Wherever two or three of you are gathered in My name, I will be there, too."

(based on John 10:1–18 and Matthew 18:30)

Thinking about Scripture

- Why do you think Jesus told this story to His friends?

APPLICATION: We Live Our Faith

Signs of Belonging

Catholics believe that Jesus is with them in each of the seven sacraments. Do you know these seven signs of belonging? Read the clues of this puzzle and write the name of each sacrament where it belongs. If the answer is more than one word, leave a space between the words.

CLUES

Across

1. A man and woman promise to love each other forever.
5. A sign of peace and healing.
6. The "door" or "gate" to the Church.
7. The Holy Spirit helps us to follow Jesus.

Down

2. God forgives someone who is sorry.
3. A man promises to serve God's Family.
4. The Body and Blood of Jesus.

APPLICATION: WE PRAY

We Belong to God's Family

Leader: In Baptism, we were called to join the Family of God. God guides us through the Ten Commandments and the Great Commandment. These rules of love show us how to live and help us make the right choices.

Reader 1: This is a reading from the First Letter to the Corinthians. Listen to Saint Paul's description of Christian love.

(Read 1 Corinthians 13:1–7, 13.)

Leader: Think about the words we heard. Then, in the heart, write your specific idea of what love is.

(Take a moment to do so.)

Reader 2: Let us pray. Love is telling the truth, even if it means getting in trouble.

All: Jesus, help us follow Your commandments to love.

Reader 3: Love is being happy for someone else's success:

All: Jesus, show us how to love as You did.

Reader 4: Love is praying about what we say and do.

All: Jesus, it is good to know You are always with us.

Reader 5: Love is doing our best.

All: Jesus, know that we will keep trying to follow You.

Leader: (Read the statements on the heart.) Dear God, You created us out of love. It is this love we will try to live, every day.

All: Amen.

Family Note: Your child's text aims to teach an understanding of our Catholic faith through our primary celebration—the Mass. Lesson 1 opens with the Greeting at Mass and relates this to the theme of "belonging." Through our Baptism, we belong to God's Family. As children of God, we are called to live as the Creator, the source of love. Pray this service with as many members of your family as possible. You will need pens or pencils to write in the heart. If it is too small of a space, have your child draw a larger heart on a plain sheet of paper.

INTRODUCTION: WE CELEBRATE

2 We Ask Forgiveness

The Penitential Rite

Priest: Coming together as God's family, with confidence let us ask the Father's forgiveness, for He is full of gentleness and compassion.

(Silent reflection)

You were sent to heal the contrite: Lord, have mercy.

People: Lord, have mercy.

Priest: You came to call sinners: Christ, have mercy.

People: Christ, have mercy.

Priest: You plead for us at the right hand of the Father: Lord, have mercy.

People: Lord, have mercy.

Priest: May almighty God have mercy on us, forgive us our sins, and bring us to everlasting life.

People: Amen.

Introduction: We Celebrate

Choosing

Daniel rushed into the library. The homework assignment was to find a certain newspaper article, read the story, and write a paragraph about it.

Daniel glanced up at the clock. Soccer practice started in just ten minutes. Quickly, Daniel raced to the stack of papers, found the right one, and located the article his teacher had assigned.

With great relief, he hurried to the copy machine. He couldn't believe his eyes. The machine had a sign that said "Out of Order." Daniel knew he'd have to copy the story by hand.

Daniel glanced at the clock again. There were only three minutes left. If he missed soccer practice, he wouldn't be able to play in Saturday's game. If he didn't do the homework assignment, he'd get in trouble in school and at home.

So Daniel made a choice. When the librarian wasn't looking, he tore out the story and put it in his pocket. Then he neatly folded the newspaper and put it back on the shelf.

Faster Might Not Be Better

The next day, Daniel was the only student who had finished the homework assignment.

"I couldn't find the story," one girl said.

"Someone tore out the article," another boy complained.

INTRODUCTION: WE CELEBRATE

All of a sudden, Daniel felt terrible. He knew he had made the wrong choice. "I have the article," he finally admitted. "I tore it out of the newspaper."

The students were silent as an unhappy frown spread over the teacher's face. "And why did you do it?" she asked quietly.

"I was in a hurry," Daniel explained.

"And was that a good reason to take the article?"

"No," Daniel admitted.

Daniel apologized to the class. He promised to return the article to the library. He promised, too, to make copies of the article for the class to read. Then the teacher and the students forgave Daniel.

Thinking about the Story

- How did Daniel's choice affect others?
- What lesson did Daniel's classmates learn?

Development: We Believe

Peace and Friendship

The Eucharist is a sign of reconciliation. The word reconciliation means "to bring together again." At Mass, Catholics pray that all members of God's family may come together in peace and friendship. They pray for an end to fighting, hatred, and all the things that separate people from one another. When Catholics receive the Body and Blood of Jesus, they celebrate their unity with and love for one another. They "become one" in the Lord Jesus.

It may be hard to imagine, but every choice you make affects other people. Because you belong to God's Family, every choice you make affects the members of God's Family. Your good choices can help build up and strengthen the bonds between the members. Your bad choices can hurt and weaken those bonds.

When Catholics gather together at Mass, they spend time during the **penitential** rite thinking about their choices. They ask God to forgive them for their bad choices. They ask the other members of the Church community for *forgiveness,* too. They ask for God's help to lead better lives.

We are not left alone when it comes to making choices. God's grace helps us to be strong and to do what is good. God's gift of *conscience,* the ability to know right from wrong, reminds us when we have done something wrong, or sinned. And the **sacrament of Reconciliation** welcomes back the sinner with God's own kindness. It gives God's grace to make good choices.

The Forgiveness of Sin

There are different types of **sin**. *Venial sin* weakens our friendship with God. A person who has committed a venial sin, and is sorry for that sin, may still receive Communion.

Mortal sin is choosing something that is very seriously wrong. A person who chooses mortal sin decides to turn away from God's love. Before receiving Communion, a person who has committed a mortal sin must turn back to God and make peace with God's Family through the sacrament of Reconciliation. Then the person can receive Communion.

In order for a sin to be mortal, the action must be seriously wrong. The person must know that the action is seriously wrong. And the person must freely choose to do the action anyway. No one can commit a mortal sin by mistake or by accident.

When we choose wrongly, when we listen to **temptation** and fall into sin, we need to remember that God is willing to forgive us. God's Family is waiting to welcome us back. We only have to show we are sorry, promise to do better, and work to make up for what we have done wrong.

We Catholics Believe

A **penitential** attitude means having sorrow for sin. People who are penitential take responsibility for their wrong choices and actions. They seriously try to change for the better.

Sin is choosing to do wrong which results in hurting our friendship with God.

In the **sacrament of Reconciliation,** a person confesses his or her sins to a priest. The person expresses sorrow for these sins and promises to do better. The priest forgives the person, in the name of God and the members of God's Family. This sacrament is also known as *Penance* and *Confession*.

Temptation is the pull we all feel toward doing what we know is wrong. Jesus showed us how to say no to temptation.

DEVELOPMENT: WE BELIEVE

Zacchaeus

Zacchaeus was a wealthy man who lived in the town of Jericho. His job was to collect taxes for the government. Zacchaeus was not very popular. Some people called him a cheater. They thought he kept the tax money for himself.

One day, Zacchaeus learned that Jesus was coming to town. He was very anxious to see this Teacher who could also work miracles. So Zacchaeus found out which street Jesus would take. When he got to the street, a great crowd had already gathered. Because Zacchaeus was very short, he could not see over the people's heads. So he climbed up the nearest tree and waited there for Jesus to arrive.

When Jesus came near the tree, He looked up and saw Zacchaeus. "Come down from there," Jesus said, "for today I must stay at your house."

Zacchaeus was delighted. He climbed down the tree as quickly as possible. But the people in the crowd grumbled and complained. "Zacchaeus is a cheat and a sinner," they said to Jesus. "How can You stay with him?"

Zacchaeus was very sad. He thought Jesus would reject him, just like everyone else. So he spoke up.

"Lord," Zacchaeus said, "I will give away half of my possessions to the poor. If I have ever cheated people, I will give them back four times what they paid me."

At this, everyone was happy. The people knew that Zacchaeus meant what he said. They would no longer judge him harshly. And from that day forward, Zacchaeus lived up to the goodness Jesus saw in him.

(based on Luke 19:1–10)

Thinking about Scripture

- What made Zacchaeus want to change his life?
- What did the people learn from the way Jesus treated Zacchaeus?

APPLICATION: WE LIVE OUR FAITH

Sin and Forgiveness

Circle the **T** if the statement is true. Circle the **F** if the statement is false.

1. You can commit a mortal sin by accident.   T   F
2. Every choice you make affects other people.   T   F
3. The word reconciliation means "to divide or separate."   T   F
4. Catholics who have committed a venial sin may not receive Communion.   T   F
5. God always loves us and is willing to forgive us.   T   F

Fill in the following chart. For each category, tell about a time you forgave someone. Then tell about a time when you needed forgiveness.

Category	I Forgave	I Was Forgiven
Family		
School		
Friends		

Vocabulary

Write your own definitions for the following words:

Sin _____

Reconciliation _____

Penance _____

Application: We Pray

Prayer Service on Forgiveness

Plan a prayer service with your family. Use these suggestions to help you choose a reading, a prayer, and an action. Write your choices in the Choices box. Then choose a time to pray this service together.

Readings:
- Matthew 5:21–26 (Forgive One Another)
- Matthew 18:21–35 (The Unforgiving Servant)
- Luke 15:11–32 (The Forgiving Father)

Prayers:

First, think about times when forgiveness is needed in family life. Write these times in the box. Then, have each person in turn read one of the times. Everyone responds, "Lord, have mercy." Finally, all pray together this prayer for forgiveness:

> My God, I am sorry for my sins with all my heart. In choosing to do wrong and failing to do good, I have sinned against You whom I should love above all things. With Your help, I will do penance, sin no more and avoid those things which lead me to make wrong choices. Jesus Christ suffered and died for us. In His name, dear Father, forgive me. Amen.

Actions:

Some possible actions that might be part of this prayer service:
- Offer one another a sign of peace and forgiveness.
- Write a penance on a piece of paper, and share it at the service.
- Think of one way you can be more forgiving with the members of your family.

CHOICES

Family Note: Lesson 2 begins with the Penitential Rite and continues with the choices people make and their need for forgiveness. Work as a family to choose the reading, prayer, and action for this prayer service on forgiving. Choose a convenient time and a comfortable place. You may wish to light a candle to remind you of God's presence.

INTRODUCTION: WE CELEBRATE

Meeting Jesus in God's Word

Liturgy of the Word

Cantor: *Alleluia!*

People: Alleluia!

Cantor: The heavens were opened and the Father's voice was heard: this is My beloved Son, hear Him. Alleluia!

People: Alleluia!

Priest: The Lord be with you.

People: And also with you.

Priest: A reading from the Gospel according to Matthew (or Mark, or Luke, or John).

People: Glory to you, Lord.

21

INTRODUCTION: WE CELEBRATE

Listening

Sunday nights in the Huston household were always the same. Mr Huston would sit in his easy chair and read the paper. Mrs. Huston would sit on the sofa and mend clothes. Angela and Ricardo, meanwhile, would quietly entertain themselves.

This Sunday night, however, Angela and Ricardo were both restless. They had finished their Halloween costumes for tomorrow night. Even their homework was done. For them, October 30 seemed like the longest evening of the year.

"Why don't you listen to the radio?" their father suggested.

"We already missed the Charlie McCarthy show," Angela pouted. "There's never anything worth listening to after that."

"Maybe there's something on the news," Mrs. Huston said.

Half-heartedly, Ricardo began moving the dial on the radio.

From Boredom to Terror!

Suddenly, a frightened voice filled the Huston living room. "Flash!" the announcer shouted. "A meteor has crashed near Grovers Mill, New Jersey. There is fire everywhere. Fifteen hundred people have already been killed."

Angela gasped with surprise. "Grovers Mill isn't far from here!" she exclaimed.

Mr. Huston put down his paper.

"No, wait!" the radio voice continued. "It's not a meteor after all! Instead, it's a flying metallic cylinder. Creatures from space have landed in Grovers Mill!"

Now, even Ricardo was frightened.

"Unbelievable as this may sound," the announcer went on, "invaders from some other world are presently flying over New Jersey. Poison gas seems to be spreading quickly. Bombs are dropping everywhere."

"We're going to die!" Mrs. Huston blurted out fearfully.

"Not if I can help it," Mr. Huston assured her. "All of you, grab your coats, and get into the car. We're getting out of here right away." That night, thousands of families throughout America thought the world was ending. Hospitals treated people for shock. Newspaper reporters rushed to New Jersey to cover the story. Hundreds of people went to church to pray. Countless others tied up the phone lines. Everyone wanted gas masks, ambulances, and police rescue squads.

If these people had only listened to the entire radio program, they would have known it was not a news broadcast. Instead, an actor named Orson Welles was dramatizing *The War of the Worlds,* a novel about Martians who come to earth. The story was only a story. There was no real-life invasion.

Thinking about the Story

- What does this story tell you about the importance of listening?

DEVELOPMENT: WE BELIEVE

Jesus Is Alive Today

Catholics know that Jesus, God's Son, is with them at Mass. They meet Jesus in the Bread and Wine of Communion. They also meet Jesus in the words of the *Gospels*.

In all, there are four Gospels—Matthew, Mark, Luke, and John. They are found in the New Testament of the Bible. Each Gospel tells about who Jesus is, what He did, and what He taught. Within the Gospels are teaching stories called **parables** that Jesus told the people.

Catholics try to listen carefully when the Scripture readings are read at Mass. They believe these readings contain the Good News—the message of God's saving love. The readings tell how God's love is stronger than sin and death. They show how God's love lasts forever.

The Word of God

Jesus is sometimes called "*the Word of God*" because He spoke God's message. Everything Jesus said and did tells about God's love. Jesus showed God's love through His **miracles** when He cured people who were blind, deaf, lame, or unable to speak. He lived God's love when He forgave sinners and made sick people feel better. Jesus showed God's love when He changed water into wine at a wedding party. He lived God's love when He hugged little children and acted kindly to those whom others had rejected.

The greatest lesson about God's love was given in the suffering and death of Jesus. Jesus offered His life as a sacrifice for all people. Jesus rose from the dead. He is with God's Family forever.

DEVELOPMENT: WE BELIEVE

Listen to Love

We need to hear God's Word and let it grow in our hearts. Listening to the stories of Jesus can help us remember how to live His Way.

A **parable** is a special story used by Jesus to teach His Way. Jesus told these stories about everyday things that were familiar to the people—seeds, fishing nets, sheep, flowers—so they would understand the message.

A **miracle** is a sign of God's power and love at work in the world. The miracles of Jesus show God's power to heal, to forgive, to nourish, and to set us free.

DEVELOPMENT: WE BELIEVE

Walking to Emmaus

Two *disciples,* or followers of Jesus, were walking the seven miles from Jerusalem to Emmaus. The road was dusty, and they were talking to each other as they went along.

Suddenly, a stranger came up to them. "What are you two talking about?" the man asked.

The two friends stopped and sadly shook their heads. "Don't you know what happened a few days ago in Jerusalem?" they asked. "Our leader, Jesus, was put to death on a cross. Today, some women went to His tomb and found it empty. Instead, they saw some angels who said that Jesus is alive. Now, we do not know what to think."

The stranger looked at the two friends. "How foolish you are!" He told them. "Jesus had to die in order to bring new life to people. This is what the prophets have always said." Then, beginning with Moses and all the prophets, the man explained what was written about the Savior.

Later, the two friends remembered all that the stranger had said. They also remembered how excited they felt when He explained to them the meaning of the Scriptures. All of a sudden, they knew who the stranger was. It was Jesus Himself! Now they knew He had really risen from the dead!

(based on Luke 24:13–35)

Thinking about Scripture

- How did listening help the disciples recognize Jesus?

APPLICATION: WE LIVE OUR FAITH

Listening to Jesus

Draw a picture abut one of the events in the life of Jesus. Then, in your own words, tell what this event says about God's love.

God's Love:
_____
_____
_____

APPLICATION: WE PRAY

The Stories of Jesus

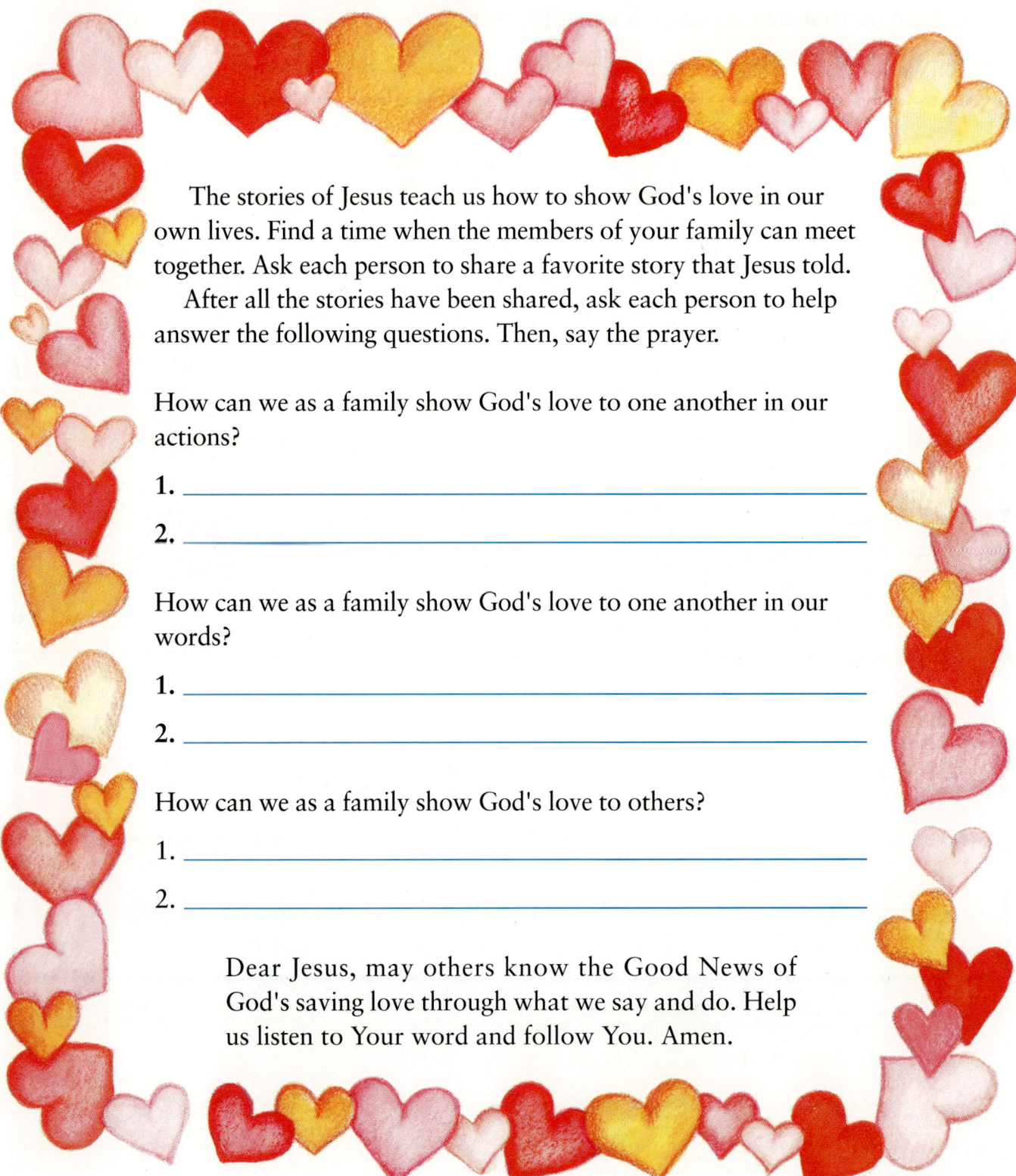

The stories of Jesus teach us how to show God's love in our own lives. Find a time when the members of your family can meet together. Ask each person to share a favorite story that Jesus told.

After all the stories have been shared, ask each person to help answer the following questions. Then, say the prayer.

How can we as a family show God's love to one another in our actions?

1. _____
2. _____

How can we as a family show God's love to one another in our words?

1. _____
2. _____

How can we as a family show God's love to others?

1. _____
2. _____

Dear Jesus, may others know the Good News of God's saving love through what we say and do. Help us listen to Your word and follow You. Amen.

Family Note: Lesson 3 focuses on the readings at Mass that tell us of the Good News of God's saving love. The importance of the activity on this page is not so much the stories themselves, but the way you listen to one another. Try to make room for storytelling in your everyday living. In simple ways, help your child see God's presence in your family.

INTRODUCTION: WE CELEBRATE

4 All That We Have

Preparation of Gifts

Priest: Blessed are You, Lord, God of all creation. Through Your goodness we have this bread to offer, which earth has given and human hands have made. It will become for us the bread of life.

People: Blessed be God forever.

Priest: Blessed are You, Lord, God of all creation. Through Your goodness we have this wine to offer, fruit of the vine and work of human hands. It will become our spiritual drink.

People: Blessed be God forever.

Giving

Right near the end of math class, Mrs. McKinley, the school principal, made an unexpected announcement.

"I just came from a meeting with the city building inspector," said Mrs. McKinley. "Our school hall does not meet safety standards. It will have to be torn down."

Clare's eyes got big. The hall was used for everything from assemblies to lunches on cold days.

The principal continued. "I need you to help raise money for a new hall. Starting today, we're going to be selling candy bars and magazine subscriptions. The student who brings in the most money will win a trip for the entire family to Disney World."

Clare got excited. Even though her parents both worked, they couldn't afford to take the family to Disney World. She really wanted to win!

So Clare began selling magazine subscriptions to her neighbors. She sold candy bars to people outside the bank and the grocery store. She gave candy bars to her parents to sell at their offices. Each night, she carefully counted the money she had collected. The amount got bigger and bigger.

At last, the final day of the contest arrived. Clare held her breath as the principal announced the results. She just knew she would win the trip!

Giving Isn't Easy

"It's not fair," Clare complained to her parents that night. "Steve Johnson is the richest kid in school. He didn't need to win the trip!"

"Even so," her father replied, "if he sold more than anyone else, he deserved to win."

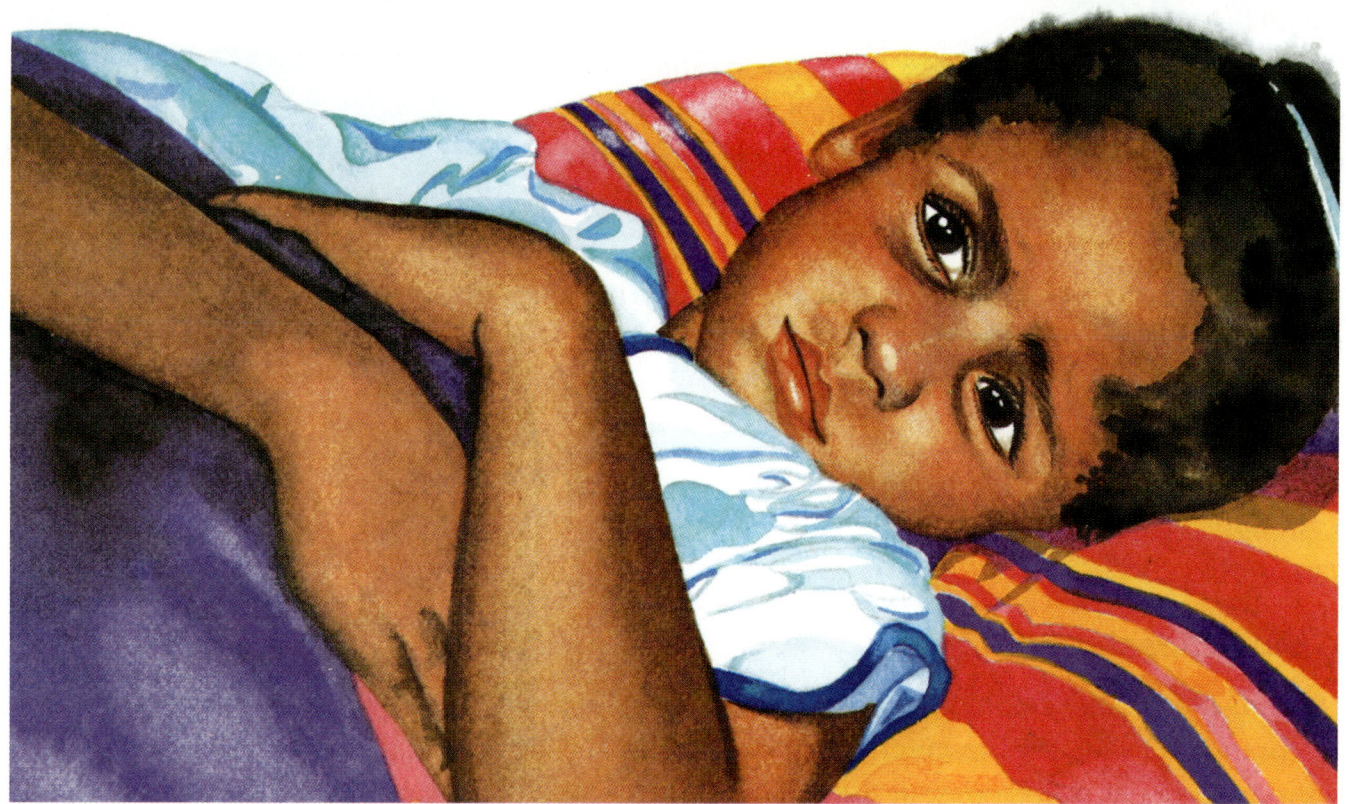

"I don't think Steve sold anything at all," Clare said. "I think his parents just wrote out a check."

"Maybe so," her mother said, "but he still turned in more money than you."

"But I worked so hard!" Clare protested. "I put in so much time!"

"Yes," her father agreed. "And when you use the new school hall, you'll see that it was worth the effort."

"You gave all that you could," her mother added. "Be proud of that."

Clare sighed and then went to her room. She thought for a long time about what her parents had said. But she still had mixed feelings. Maybe, she thought, giving is not always as easy as it seems.

Thinking about the Story

- Why did Clare want to help raise money in the first place?
- What were some things she learned about giving?

DEVELOPMENT: WE BELIEVE

Gifts Given

Everyone in God's Family has been given gifts. Some gifts include the ability to sing, to dance, or to play a musical instrument. Other gifts include a humble heart, a cheerful outlook, and the willingness to learn.

In some ways these gifts from God are similar to the gifts we get from people. Think about some gifts you have gotten from people who love you. You probably liked showing these gifts to others, because the best gifts are meant to be shared, and not hidden away.

The same is true for the gifts God gives you. You show your appreciation for them by using them and sharing them with others.

Giving Ourselves

Gifts play an important part in the Eucharistic celebration. During the Presentation of Gifts, bread and wine are brought to the priest at the altar. The bread and wine remind Catholics of all the gifts God has given us. The bread and wine also tell us that it is important to share and to give. We know that giving is not always easy and that **sacrifice** is often needed. Jesus showed us this.

There are many ways in which the members of God's Family give gifts of themselves. Each of these ways is known as a **ministry.** Some ministries are associated with the Eucharist. Greeters welcome people to church, and lectors read Scripture. Music ministers choose songs, lead the singing, and play musical instruments. Altar servers assist the priest, and Eucharistic ministers give out Communion at Mass or take Communion to the sick.

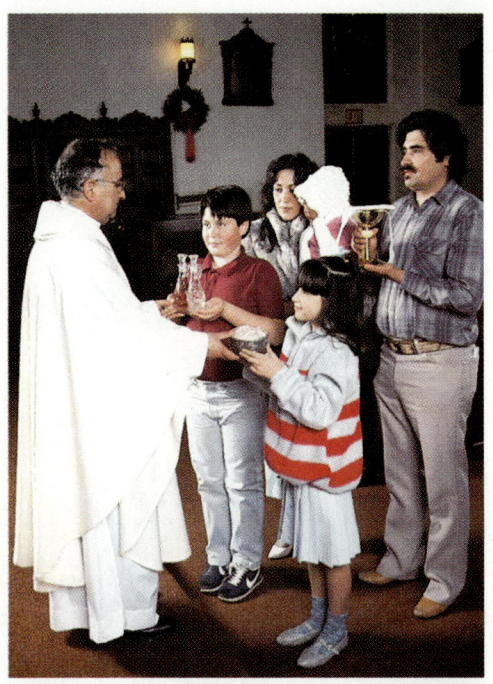

There are ways to minister to others outside of the Eucharist as well. **Parish** members and organizations share their time, talents, and money to help those in need.

We Catholics Believe

To **sacrifice** means to offer or give up something for another's good. Jesus offered Himself to God as a sacrifice for our good. The Mass is the perfect sacrifice. At Mass, we offer ourselves with Jesus to the Father.

Ministry is another word for service. People who help others in the Family of God are said to have a ministry—a special call to serve others in some way.

A **parish** is a community of Catholics who gather and worship together. The parish is usually led by a pastor and is served by many parish ministers.

Development: We Believe

The Widow's Coins

One day, Jesus and His friends sat down by the doorway to the great Temple of Jerusalem. They watched as people approached the Temple door. Before entering, many people dropped money into the Temple offering box. Rich people dressed in fine clothes dropped in large sums of money. A poor widow also came along. She dropped in two small coins worth a few cents.

When Jesus saw this widow, He smiled. He said to His friends, "Do you realize she put in more than all the other people we have seen? All the rich people gave something they could afford. They will not miss what they gave away. But that woman has just given away every penny she had."

(based on Mark 12:41–44)

Thinking about Scripture

- Why did Jesus say that the widow gave more than anyone else?
- In what way is the widow like Jesus?

APPLICATION: WE LIVE OUR FAITH

Sharing Our Gifts

Match each person in column A with the ministry in column B.

A

_____ 1. Eucharistic minister

_____ 2. Lector

_____ 3. Music minister

_____ 4. Presenter of Gifts

_____ 5. Greeter

_____ 6. Catechist

_____ 7. Altar server

B

a. Leads the singing at Mass.

b. Teaches others about Jesus.

c. Gives out Communion.

d. Welcomes people to church.

e. Reads scripture at Mass.

f. Helps the priest during Mass.

g. Brings the bread and wine to the priest.

Fill in the following chart. List three gifts, or talents, God has given you. Then tell one way you can share each gift with others.

My Gifts

1. _____

2. _____

3. _____

Sharing My Gifts

_____

_____

_____

Vocabulary

Write your own definitions for the following words:

Ministry _____

Sacrifice _____

Parish _____

35

APPLICATION: WE PRAY

Praise God for Gifts

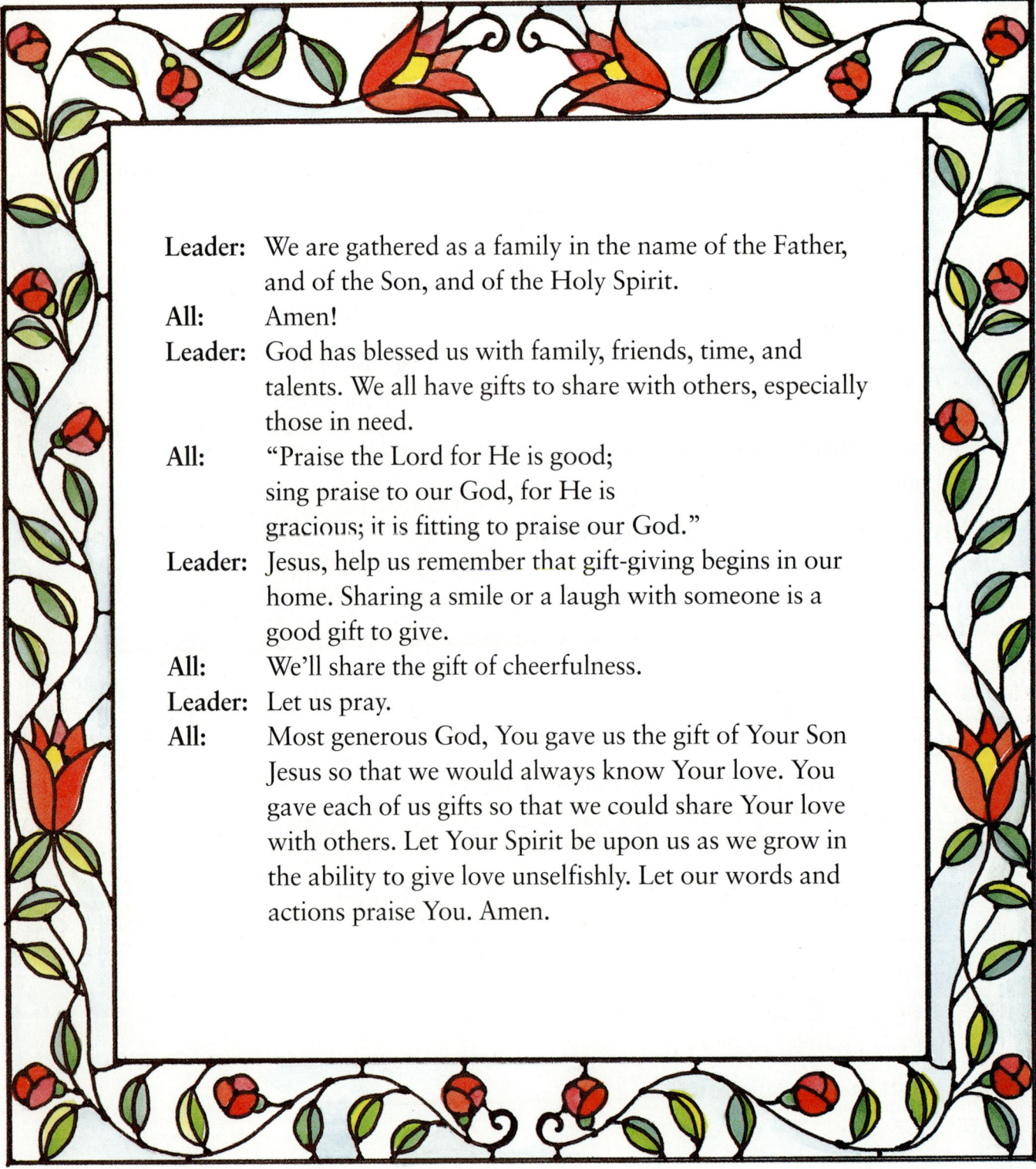

Leader: We are gathered as a family in the name of the Father, and of the Son, and of the Holy Spirit.
All: Amen!
Leader: God has blessed us with family, friends, time, and talents. We all have gifts to share with others, especially those in need.
All: "Praise the Lord for He is good; sing praise to our God, for He is gracious; it is fitting to praise our God."
Leader: Jesus, help us remember that gift-giving begins in our home. Sharing a smile or a laugh with someone is a good gift to give.
All: We'll share the gift of cheerfulness.
Leader: Let us pray.
All: Most generous God, You gave us the gift of Your Son Jesus so that we would always know Your love. You gave each of us gifts so that we could share Your love with others. Let Your Spirit be upon us as we grow in the ability to give love unselfishly. Let our words and actions praise You. Amen.

Family Note: Lesson 4 opens with the Preparation of the Gifts at Mass and proceeds to talk about using the gifts God has blessed us with. As a follow through to this prayer service, your family may wish to decide on a specific gift to give to someone in need. Perhaps you can make a meal for a sick neighbor, call a friend or relative who needs some cheer, or gather a box of clothing for a shelter for the homeless.

INTRODUCTION: WE CELEBRATE

Remember and Give Thanks

Eucharistic Prayer II for Children

Priest: The Lord be with you.

People: And also with you.

Priest: Lift up your hearts.

People: We lift them up to the Lord.

Priest: Let us give thanks to the Lord our God.

People: It is right to give God thanks and praise.

People: **Hosanna** in the highest.

Priest: Because You love us, You gave us this great and beautiful world. With Jesus we sing Your praise.

People: **Hosanna** in the highest.

Priest: For such great love we thank You with the angels and saints as they praise You and sing.

People: Holy, holy, holy Lord, God of power and might. Heaven and earth are full of Your glory. Hosanna in the highest. Blessed is He who comes in the name of the Lord. Hosanna in the highest.

37

Introduction: We Celebrate

Remembering

"Our family reunion is the same weekend as the Boy Scout camping trip!" Davey Butler said, rather upset.

"Well, you can set up your tent in Grandma and Grandpa's backyard," Mr. Butler answered.

"It won't be the same!" Davey protested. "Besides, at the family reunion, there will be just a bunch of grown-ups sitting around, talking and eating."

"Those 'grown-ups' are your relatives," Mr. Butler pointed out. "And you can always play with your cousins."

"But the only cousins I have are girls," Davey argued.

"I know you're disappointed," Davey's Dad said. "But you're going to the reunion."

One month later, Davey went with his Dad to the Butler farm. He felt a little awkward. He didn't always know what to say. But he rode horses with his cousins. He swam in the pond, helped Grandma gather eggs, and listened to Uncle Herb's stories.

The reunion went just as Davey had expected. This year, however, Grandpa showed some home movies Davey had never seen before.

"Who's that?" Davey asked as a Christmas scene appeared on the screen.

"That's your Dad and your Aunt Charlotte when they were about your age," Grandma answered.

The scene shifted, and Davey saw himself when he was four. He and his Dad were shoveling snow off the driveway.

"I remember that day!" Davey exclaimed. "It was really cold, and when we finished, Dad made donuts and fixed me a big cup of hot chocolate."

All the relatives laughed and shared memories of other scenes in Grandpa's movies.

A Surprise Ending

When the weekend was over, Davey and his Dad said good-bye to everyone and left for their own home.

"Thanks," Davey said as they drove toward the city. "I'm glad I went to the reunion."

"What made you change your mind?" Mr. Butler asked.

Davey thought about Grandpa's home movies and the day, years ago, when his Dad had made donuts. "I had fun," he answered simply. "It was a weekend I'll never forget."

Then Davey smiled to himself. He would never let his Dad forget the weekend, either. Someday, soon, he planned on asking his Dad to make donuts again.

Think about the Story

- Why would Davey never forget the reunion weekend?
- What did he learn from Grandpa's movies?

Development: We Believe

Do This in Memory of Me

You have learned that the Eucharist is a sign of belonging to God's Family. It is also a time of forgiveness and of listening to God's message in Scripture. At Mass, Catholics can praise God for all the gifts they have been given and offer these same gifts with Jesus to God.

A Time to Remember

The Eucharist is all these things and more. The Eucharist is also a time of remembering. During the Eucharistic Prayer at Mass, we remember the many different people who make up God's family. We pray for the pope and the *bishops,* all the priests and *deacons,* all the men and women religious. We remember the lay people who minister in the Church. We remember all the living, especially ourselves and those gathered together with us at Mass. We remember Mary, the Mother of Jesus, and Joseph, her husband. We recall the *Apostles,* the *martyrs,* the saints, and all those who have died believing in Jesus.

Time to Give Thanks

In the Eucharistic Prayer, we also remember the life, death, and resurrection of Jesus, especially what Jesus said and did at the **Last Supper.** At Mass, the priest does the same. Like Jesus, the priest blesses **unleavened bread** and wine. He says the same words Jesus said, "This is My Body. This is My Blood." He does these things in memory of Jesus.

The Eucharistic Prayer is sometimes known as the Great Prayer of Thanksgiving. In this prayer, we thank God for all that we have been given. We thank God for sending Jesus to be our **Savior.** We thank God for calling us to be members of His Family. But most of all, we thank God because we know that Jesus is really with us in the blessed Bread and Wine.

We Catholics Believe

The word **hosanna** means "to shout with joy to the Lord." Catholics say "Hosanna" during Mass because they remember that Jesus is the Savior, and they give thanks for His love.

The **Last Supper** is the special meal Jesus shared with His Apostles the night before He died. At the Last Supper, Jesus changed bread and wine into His own Body and Blood. He told His disciples to "Do this in memory of Me."

Unleavened bread is bread that contains no yeast. When the Israelites left Egypt, they could not wait for bread to rise. So, they ate only unleavened bread. Today, the Eucharistic Bread at Mass is unleavened bread.

The **Passover** is the Jewish feast of the Unleavened Bread that remembers the time God led the Israelites out of slavery to freedom. Jewish people celebrate this feast every spring with a special meal called "Seder."

Jesus is a name that means "savior." A **savior** is someone who frees others from danger or trouble. Jesus is our Savior because He freed us from sin.

Development: We Believe

The Last Supper

It was the first day of the Feast of the Unleavened Bread. That night, Jesus and His friends gathered at a house in Jerusalem.

They ate the roast lamb and the other special foods that had been prepared. They remembered the story of the **Passover**—when God's angel passed over the houses of the Israelites, and helped them escape from slavery in Egypt.

After the meal, Jesus took some bread and prayed the ancient words of blessing over it. Then, He broke the bread and gave it to His friends. "Take and eat," He said. "This is My Body."

Jesus took a cup of wine and gave thanks to God. He passed the cup around, saying, "Drink from this cup, all of you. This is the cup of My Blood. It will be shed for many people, for the forgiveness of sins."

Jesus' friends did not completely understand what He meant. But they knew this meal was special. They ate the bread and drank from the cup. Then, they sang a hymn and followed Jesus out to the Mount of Olives to pray.

(based on Mark 14:22–26)

Thinking about Scripture

- Why do you think Jesus chose bread and wine as signs of His presence?

APPLICATION: WE LIVE OUR FAITH

A Memory Help

To help you remember what you have learned in Lesson 5, fill in this puzzle. Read the clues that are given. Then write the correct answer where it belongs. If the answer is more than one word, leave a space between the words.

CLUES

Down

1. The Jewish Feast that recalls the time God led the israelites out of Egypt.
2. The Mother of Jesus.
4. The special meal Jesus shared with His friends on the night before He died.
5. The husband of Mary.
6. At Mass, Catholics _____ the life, death, and resurrection of Jesus.
7. A word that means "shout with joy to the Lord."
9. Jesus changed this into His own Blood.

Across

3. Twelve special friends of Jesus.
8. The leaders of Catholics in a group of parishes.
10. The part of the Mass when we remember the Last Supper and give thanks for God's love.
11. Jesus changed this into His own Body.
12. The human leader of all Roman Catholics in the world.
13. This bread contains no yeast.
14. What the word Jesus means.

43

APPLICATION: WE PRAY

Family Reminders

Remembering is important for God's Family and for your family, too. In the spaces below, write down five events your family considers to be important. These events might be a wedding day, the birth of a baby, a new job, the death of a family member, a special trip—whatever your family particularly remembers.

Important Family Events

1. _____
2. _____
3. _____
4. _____
5. _____

Talk about the choices and why they are considered important. Did they change your lives? Did they add joy? Did they bring loss or pain?

End with this prayer.

> Heavenly Father, our family has remembered some important times in our lives. They changed us in some way. We want to remember that You are always with us—in the ordinary everyday happenings and in the special events we'll never forget. Like the truest friend, You are with us in good times and in bad, in happy moments and in sad. We thank You for Your constant presence. Amen.

Family Note: Lesson 5 opens with the Eucharistic Prayer which tells us that the Mass is a time for remembering. The activity on this page focuses on remembering, too. If any of the family-history events you list involve loss or sadness, take special care to remind your child that Jesus also experienced such emotions, and He is with us at all times.

INTRODUCTION: WE CELEBRATE

6 Give Us This Day

The Lord's Prayer

Priest: Let us pray with confidence to the Father in the words our Savior gave us.

People: Our Father, who art in heaven, hallowed be Thy name. Thy kingdom come, Thy will be done on earth as it is in heaven. Give us this day our daily bread; and forgive us our trespasses as we forgive those who trespass against us; and lead us not into temptation, but deliver us from evil.

Priest: Deliver us, Lord, from every evil, and grant us peace in our day. In Your mercy keep us free from sin and protect us from all anxiety as we wait in joyful hope for the coming of our Savior, Jesus Christ.

People: For the kingdom, the power, and the glory are Yours, now and forever.

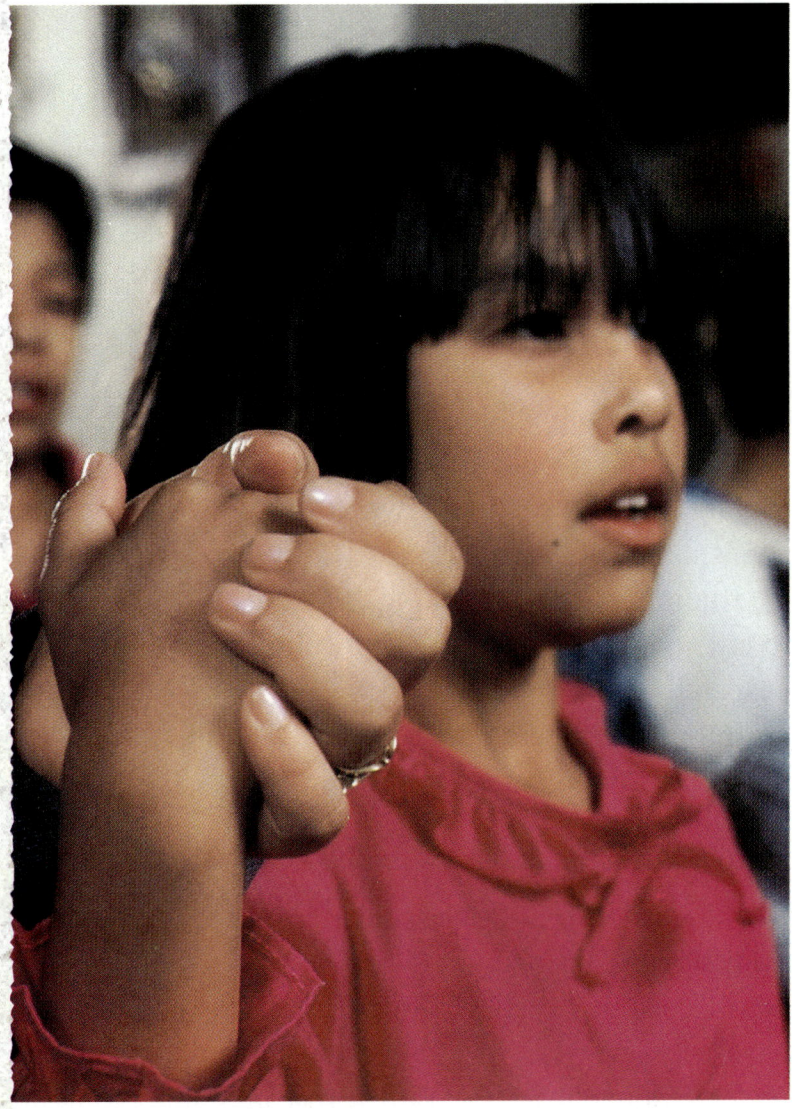

45

Introduction: We Celebrate

Asking

Solomon was feeling both sad and very afraid. Tomorrow he would be crowned King of Israel. He would rule from the throne which had once belonged to his father, David. Solomon didn't know if he were ready for such responsibility. David had been a very good king, and the people had loved him. It would be hard for anyone to take his place.

That night, God appeared to Solomon in a dream. "Ask something of Me," God said. "And I will give you that one thing."

Solomon thought and thought before he answered. Since he could only ask for one thing, he wanted to make sure that he asked for something good. "Perhaps I should ask for a long life," Solomon thought to himself. "But what good is a long life if that life is not happy?"

"Perhaps I should ask for riches," Solomon continued to think. "But why should I want riches that my enemies could someday steal?"

Solomon kept on thinking. "Perhaps I should ask God to kill all my enemies. At least then my life would be peaceful."

But none of these wishes seemed like the best thing. Finally, Solomon made his decision.

The Decision

"O Lord, my God," he said, "You have made me, Your servant, king to follow my father David. But I am still young. I do not know how to act. Since I may have only one wish, I ask that You give me a wise and understanding heart. For only a wise and understanding king will be able to judge Your people and to know right from wrong."

INTRODUCTION: WE CELEBRATE

God was very pleased that Solomon had asked for wisdom and understanding. So God said, "Because you have asked for this—and not for a long life for yourself, nor for riches, nor for the life of your enemies—I will do as you have asked. I will make you the wisest person who has ever lived. In addition, I will give you great riches and make you famous. And, if you keep My commandments, I will also give you a long life."

When Solomon awoke from his dream, he went to Jerusalem. There, he gave offerings to God and a banquet for all his servants.

(based on 1 Kings 3:4–14)

Thinking about Scripture

- Why was it important for Solomon to think before he asked God for a gift?

Development: We Believe

Public Prayer

You talk and listen to other people every day. Such talking and listening is called communication. **Prayer** is a special kind of communication. Whenever you talk to God or listen to what God is saying, you are praying.

Basically, prayer is any act of showing love for God. Private prayer can be anything you think, do, or say in private to communicate with God. Public prayer, or **liturgy,** is the Church's public worship of God and includes the Mass and the sacraments.

Everything that happens at Mass is a prayer! Sometimes certain prayers—such as the Glory to God or the Lord's Prayer—are prayed aloud by the whole congregation. Sometimes the priest says a prayer alone, and the people answer "**Amen.**" At other times, praying occurs in song and music. Prayer also takes the form of actions—**genuflecting,** standing, sitting, or kneeling. Finally, there are times for silent prayer as well.

Not only are there different ways to pray, there are four different kinds of prayer. All of them are prayed during Mass. The members of God's Family *praise* God because of His goodness and blessings. They express *sorrow* for their sins. They *thank* God for all that they have been given. And they ask, or *petition,* God for what they need.

Prayer of Petition

During the Prayer of the Faithful at Mass, the community petitions God to meet the physical and spiritual needs of the people. In the Eucharistic Prayer, God is asked to give the members of His family greater love, forgiveness, unity, and peace. And during the Lord's Prayer, everyone prays, "give us this day our daily bread," admitting how much they depend on God. They know that God will give them every good thing.

Being a Pray-er

Although one way of praying is to ask God for something, that is not what prayer is. Rather, prayer is the way we answer God's call to grow in love. Prayer doesn't make God care about us. God already cares about us. Prayer helps us to know and love God. By knowing and loving God, we grow in our love for others.

We Catholics Believe

The word **liturgy** means the "work of the people." In liturgy, we use more than words. We also pray with our bodies, by the gestures and actions we use.

The word **Amen** means "Yes, I agree," or "Let it be so." When Catholics say "Amen" at the end of a prayer, they are agreeing with what was said in the prayer. The **Great Amen** at Mass is the people's way of saying yes to all that was said during the Eucharistic Prayer.

To **genuflect** is to kneel on one knee. In the days when knights wore heavy armor, they could not bow before the king, or they would tip over. If they tried to kneel, they could not get back up again! So they genuflected to the king. When we genuflect, we are showing that Jesus is our King.

Development: We Believe

The Two Friends

One day, the people asked Jesus to talk about prayer. So Jesus said, "Suppose it is midnight, and you go to the house of your best friend. You knock on the door and say, 'Friend, lend me three loaves of bread. Relatives have just arrived from out of town, and I have nothing to offer them.' But the friend inside the house replies, 'Go away and do not bother me. I've already gone to bed. I'm too tired to get up and give you anything.'"

Jesus continued. "Now you have a choice. You can apologize to your friend and leave empty-handed, or you can knock on your friend's door again. I tell you, if you knock long enough, your friend will get up. You will get the bread you want, simply because you kept making so much noise."

The people nodded their heads in agreement. But they didn't understand what the story had to do with prayer.

So Jesus explained the story. "When you pray, ask God to give you what you need. Seek the answers to your questions. Keep knocking on God's door. For everyone who asks, receives. Everyone who seeks, finds. And to everyone who knocks, the door will be opened."

(based on Luke 11:5–10)

Thinking about Scripture

- What do you think this story has to do with prayer?

APPLICATION: WE LIVE OUR FAITH

Types of Prayer

Choose the type of prayer in column B which best matches the example in column A.

A

_____ 1. Glory to God in the highest!
_____ 2. Jesus, help me.
_____ 3. Thank You, God, for my family.
_____ 4. Give us this day our daily bread.
_____ 5. O God, I am sorry for having done wrong.
_____ 6. Give thanks to the Lord whose love is everlasting.
_____ 7. Our Father, who art in heaven, hallowed be Thy name.
_____ 8. Have mercy on me, for I have sinned.

B

a. Praise
b. Thanksgiving
c. Petition
d. Sorrow for sin

What does Jesus' story about the two friends mean to you?

_____
_____
_____

Vocabulary

Write your own definitions for the following words:

Private prayer _____

Liturgy _____

Amen _____

51

APPLICATION: WE PRAY

A Prayer Service of Petition

Here is a different type of prayer service that you can use with your family.

1. Read one of these Scripture stories:

    _____ Matthew 6:5–8 (Teaching About Prayer)
    _____ Matthew 7:7–11 (Ask and You Will Receive)
    _____ Luke 18:1–8 (The Persistent Widow)

2. Tell about a time when God answered one of your prayers.

3. Together, list five family needs or concerns that you want to pray about.

    Family Needs

    a. _____
    b. _____
    c. _____
    d. _____
    e. _____

4. Referring to your list, write a family prayer asking God to give your family what it needs. Pray it together.

    Family Prayer

Family Note: Lesson 6 opens with the Lord's Prayer and expands to the ways we pray at Mass and in daily life. Ask your child to tell you the four types of prayers. In doing this page, let the family prayer be as simple and direct as you can. It need not be overly solemn or wordy. You may wish to display it in a prominent place.

INTRODUCTION: WE CELEBRATE

The Bread of Life

Communion

Priest: This is the Lamb of God, who takes away the sins of the world. Happy are those who are called to His Supper.

People: Lord, I am not worthy to receive you, but only say the word and I shall be healed.

Priest: The Body of Christ.

People: Amen.

Priest: The Blood of Christ.

People: Amen.

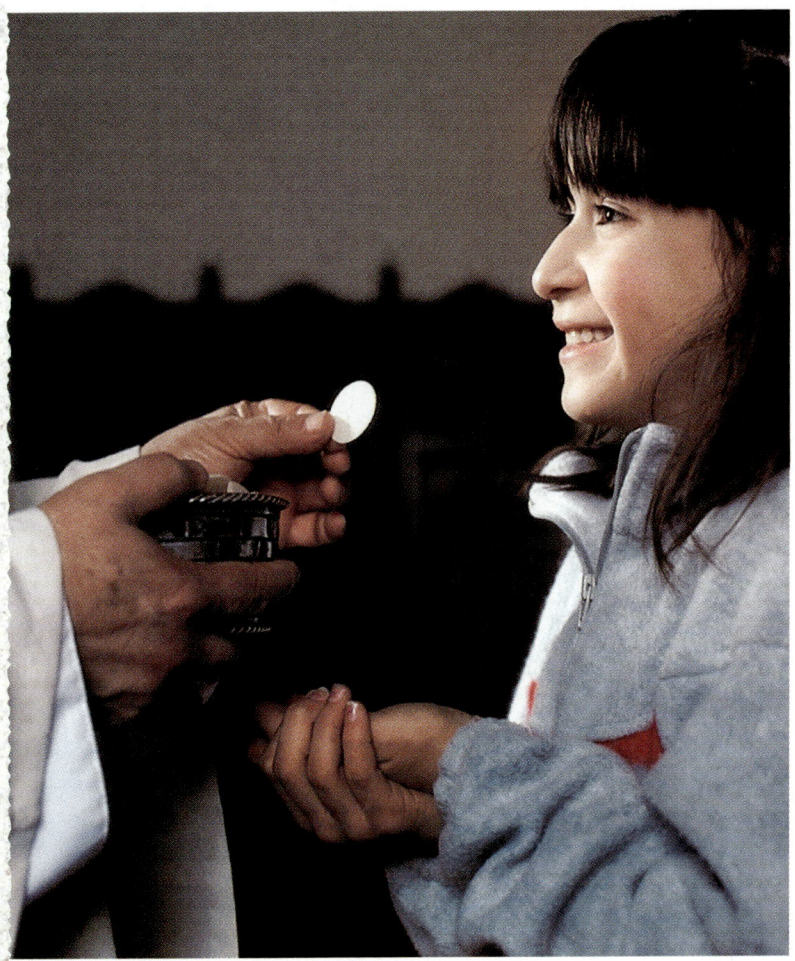

Introduction: We Celebrate

Sharing

Aunt Myra and Uncle Albert were coming from out of town. Jessica Hansen insisted on cooking dinner all by herself.

It was still morning. There seemed to be plenty of time. She was proud of the menu she had planned: a salad with carrots and celery, rolls, fried chicken, mashed potatoes, green beans, and apple pie. Jessica had made each of these items before. But she had never made them all together for the same meal.

With determination, she set to work. She grated the carrots and diced the celery. She kneaded the bread dough and cleaned the chicken. She boiled the potatoes and put the string beans in a pot. She cut up apples and rolled out the pie crust.

The day passed quickly. Different members of the Hansen family asked if they could help, but Jessica refused them. She wanted to prove she could cook the dinner on her own.

At five o'clock, Aunt Myra and Uncle Albert arrived. An hour later, everyone was eagerly waiting for Jessica to put the food on the table. It was then that Jessica made a horrible discovery. The salad was mushy. The rolls looked like she had forgotten to put yeast in them. The mashed potatoes turned out lumpy. The string beans were cold. And the fried chicken was burned to a crisp! Even though she had tried her best, the dinner was ruined.

Jessica wanted to cry. She was very embarrassed.

To the Rescue

"Don't worry," Mrs. Hansen said. "There's a batch of Grandma's spaghetti sauce in the freezer. We can make pasta."

Jessica's big sister Jill went to the store for a loaf of French bread. Her brother Brad offered to start heating the water to boil the noodles.

54

Aunt Myra and Uncle Albert volunteered to make a green salad.

A half-hour later, everyone sat down to dinner. They ate pasta, salad, and garlic bread. For dessert, they ate the apple pie Jessica had made. Everyone but Jessica laughed and had a good time.

Later that night, Aunt Myra told Jessica that the pie was delicious.

"Thanks," Jessica replied sadly. "I just wish the rest of the dinner had turned out as well."

"That dinner was the best one we've had in ages!" her aunt exclaimed. "Sharing in the work was fun. And, besides, it made us feel more at home."

Jessica was surprised. Her aunt was right. Sharing in the work had been more fun and easier than doing it alone.

Thinking about the Story

- Why did Jessica refuse any help when she first made dinner?
- What did she learn from her experience?

Development: We Believe

God's Family Meal

The Eucharist is the special meal of God's Family. In some ways, the Eucharist is similar to the meals you have with your family at home. There is a table, covered with a cloth. There are dishes, and of course, there is food, too.

But the Eucharist is not an ordinary meal. The meals you eat at home feed your body. The meal of God's Family feeds your spirit.

The Table and Dishes

The table on which the Mass is celebrated is called the *altar*. It is a reminder of the altar in the Temple of Jerusalem, where the people's offerings were sacrificed to God. In the Eucharist, Jesus is our sacrifice. On the altar are lit *candles* that are a sign that Jesus is the Light of the World.

The cup that holds the wine is called a *chalice*. The plate for the bread is called a *paten*. The container used to hold the people's Communion Bread, or *hosts*, is called a *ciborium*. These dishes are beautifully made. They are often lined with gold or other precious metals.

During the Mass, the priest may sometimes put a stiff, cloth-covered card over the chalice. This cover is called a *pall*. The pall keeps anything from accidently falling into the chalice.

The priest may also spread a square napkin over the altar table. This napkin is called a *corporal*, from the Latin word for "body." The priest places the Bread, the Body of Christ, on this corporal.

The small bottles that hold the water and wine used at Mass are called *cruets*. The special place where the Eucharist is kept is called a *tabernacle*. This is the same word the Israelites used for "the place where we meet God." The tabernacle, and the lamp that is kept burning beside it at all times, are reminders that Jesus is always with His people in the Eucharist.

The Food

The word communion means "one with." Receiving *Communion* means you are one with Jesus. It also means you are one with the other members of God's family.

In Holy Communion, Jesus invites you to follow Him. He invites you to be healed of the things that bother you. He also asks you to show that you are an active member of God's Family. Sharing the Body and Blood of Jesus at Mass tells others that you are trying your best to live as Jesus did.

We Catholics Believe

The special clothes worn by the priest and other ministers during the Mass are called **vestments.** They often have signs and symbols of our faith.

During the time when the Roman empire persecuted people for following Jesus, Christians used secret signs to help other Christians know who they were. One of these signs was the outline of a **fish.** Christians marked this sign on their doorways or wore pins or pendants in the shape of fish. They did this because, in Greek, the first letters of the words "Jesus Christ, God's Son, Savior" spell the word fish. Fish are often found on the vestments, cloths, and banners used in church.

DEVELOPMENT: WE BELIEVE

Jesus Feeds the People

Wherever He went, Jesus cured many people who were sick. Soon, large crowds began to follow Him. They hoped to see Jesus work a miracle. They wanted to hear what He had to say.

One day, Jesus sat down with His friends on a hillside. When He looked up, He saw many people coming. "Where can we buy enough food for them to eat?" Jesus asked His friends.

Philip shook his head. "It would take two hundred days' wages to pay for enough food!"

Then Andrew, the brother of Peter, spoke up. "There's a boy here who has five barley loaves and two fish. But they won't feed this many people."

Jesus thought for a while. Then He had His disciples tell the people to sit down. There were about five thousand people in all. But everyone found a place to sit on the grass.

Jesus asked the boy if he would share his lunch. The boy agreed. Jesus took the five loaves, gave thanks to God, and passed them to the people nearest Him. He did the same thing with the boy's two fish. The people took the bread and the fish and shared it among themselves. They ate until they were full.

When everyone had eaten, Jesus told His disciples to gather up any food that remained. So the disciples collected the leftovers. They filled up twelve baskets with bread! When the people saw this, they were amazed. They knew they had seen a great miracle.

(based on Mark: 6:34–44)

Thinking about Scripture

- What do you think the people learned from the miracle of the bread and fish?

APPLICATION: WE LIVE OUR FAITH

At the Lord's Table
On the altar, draw the following special items that are used at the Eucharist:

candles   chalice   paten   ciborium   two cruets   coporal

Vocabulary
Tell what each of the following terms means to you as a member of God's Family:

Holy Communion

Lamb of God _____

Fish _____

APPLICATION: WE PRAY

Why Food?

What's a peach without its fuzz? What's a steak without its sizzle? What's bread without its aroma? Food doesn't limit its appeal to our sense of taste; it speaks to all of our senses. Because it can cause so many emotional and physical responses, food nourishes both body and spirit.

Jesus knew the incredible nourishing power of food, and so He chose bread and wine as the means by which we remember Him and become one with Him. He, as our Bread of Life, nourishes us in body and soul.

You might want to step back in time and sample a food that was enjoyed by Jesus and His family. Here is a simple recipe for unleavened bread that takes about 20 minutes to make, from start to finish. As you work together, make your actions a prayer to God, the source of all our bounty.

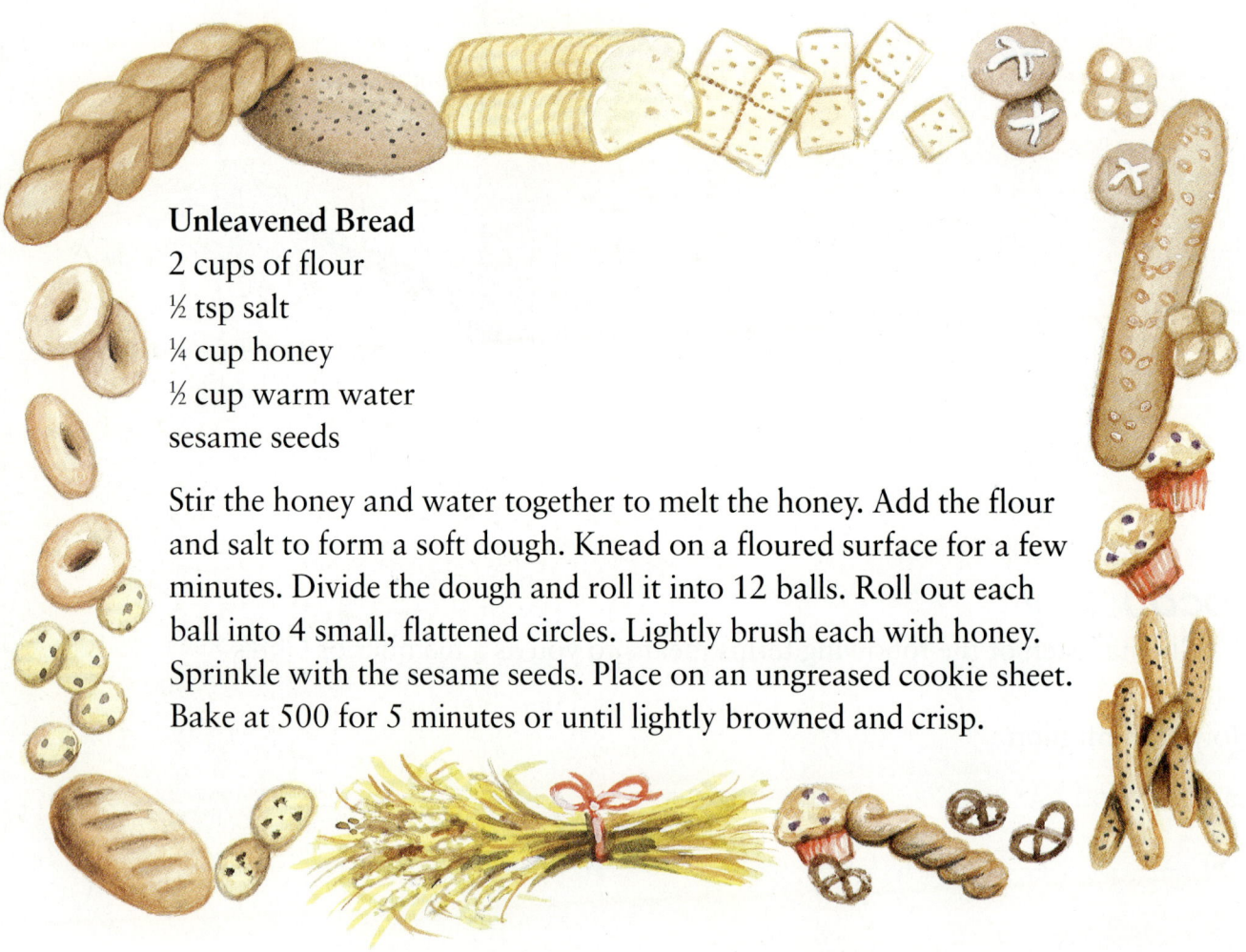

Unleavened Bread
2 cups of flour
½ tsp salt
¼ cup honey
½ cup warm water
sesame seeds

Stir the honey and water together to melt the honey. Add the flour and salt to form a soft dough. Knead on a floured surface for a few minutes. Divide the dough and roll it into 12 balls. Roll out each ball into 4 small, flattened circles. Lightly brush each with honey. Sprinkle with the sesame seeds. Place on an ungreased cookie sheet. Bake at 500 for 5 minutes or until lightly browned and crisp.

Family Note: Lesson 7 focuses on Communion as the special Meal of God's Family. Your child learned the names of the objects placed on the altar and used during Eucharist. Ask your child to name them for you when you're at Mass together. After your child receives First Communion, try to receive Communion every week together.

INTRODUCTION: WE CELEBRATE

8 Love One Another

Concluding Rite

Priest: The Lord be with you.

People: And also with you.

Priest: May almighty God bless you: the Father, and the Son, and the Holy Spirit.

People: Amen.

Priest: The Mass is ended, go in peace.

People: Thanks be to God.

Introduction: We Celebrate

Helping

Jean Donovan was just like any other girl who grew up in Ohio. She loved to ride horses and to sing. She enjoyed dating and going to parties. She also loved her Catholic faith.

After college, Jean got a job in the business world. She was very successful. But she didn't feel that she was really helping others as Jesus wanted. Then, she heard that the Archdiocese of Cincinnati was looking for **lay missionaries** to go to El Salvador. Jean gave up her job and trained to be a missionary.

In El Salvador, she worked with Maryknoll Mission sisters and with the local Catholics. She taught religion classes, helped in the medical clinic, and distributed food to the poor. She especially enjoyed caring for the children.

A War-Torn Country

The 1970s were a time of civil war in El Salvador. Different groups were struggling to attain power in the country. Some were trying to help the people have a better life. The people who wanted power accused the missionaries of taking sides against the government. During this time, many missionaries were imprisoned, kidnapped, or killed.

Jean knew that she was in a dangerous situation. But she believed this was the way she could answer Jesus' call to serve others. On a brief holiday, Jean visited some friends in Ireland. They tried to tell her not to back to El Salvador. But Jean only said, "I have to go. Who will help the children if I don't?"

On December 4, 1980, Jean Donovan and three of the sisters she worked with were found murdered by the side of a road in El Salvador.

All over the world, ordinary people follow Jesus and help build God's kingdom. Some leave their homes and go to far-off countries. Some work with needy people right next door. Some give of their time and their talents, and a few give their lives. What is most important is the fact that everyone, even the young and the old, can do something to bring justice and love in the world.

Thinking about the Story

- How did Jean Donovan follow Jesus?
- How do you follow Jesus?

Development: We Believe

Showing Love, Making Peace

Catholics know that the love, peace, and oneness they find at Mass cannot end there. As followers of Jesus, they must love and care for others in their daily lives. They must try to put an end to fighting, hatred, and selfishness. They must try to be at peace with all people.

Peace and Justice

The word peace has many meanings. "To have peace," the prophet Isaiah explained, "you must live justly." There are many ways that the followers of Jesus work for peace and justice. They try to treat others with fairness, openess, and honesty. They forgive others. They pray for their enemies. They practice love in action. They work toward world peace by keeping peace with their own families, friends, and neighbors.

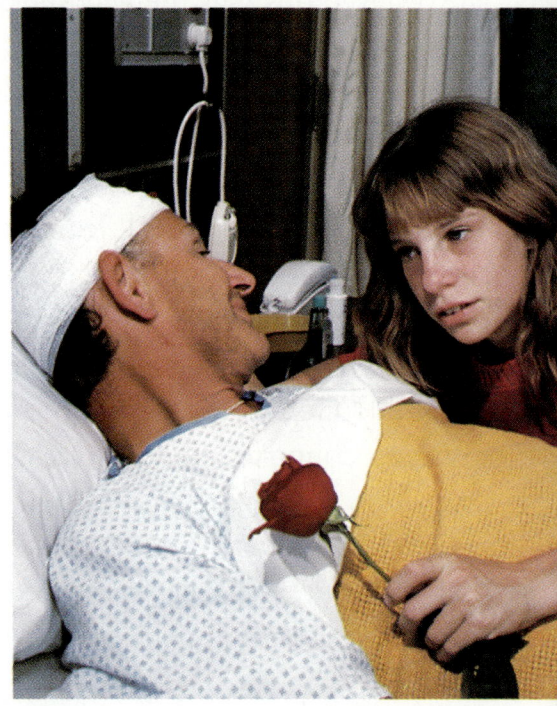

Members of God's Family also help others. They try to help all other people who are in need or in trouble. They feed the hungry and give drinks to the thirsty, cloth the naked, and shelter the homeless. They visit the sick and those in prison. They bury the dead and comfort those

who lost a loved one. These ways of helping are called the **Works of Mercy.** All followers of Jesus are called to help others in these ways.

You Can Help

In your own life, there are many ways you can help others. You can help with family chores. You can be a peacemaker on the school playground. You can reach out to someone who's lonely or left out.

Helping others is not always easy. That is why God gives us a special Helper. God's Holy Spirit comes to us in the sacrament of Baptism and is again celebrated in the sacrament of **Confirmation.** This Spirit is a spirit of love, peace, and oneness. The Holy Spirit helps the followers of Jesus to put the Eucharist into action in their daily lives. God's Spirit helps people to keep on working for peace and helping others.

Helping is a sign of love. Jesus said, "Whatever you do for others, you do for Me." Serving others is a way to show your love for them, and it is a way to show your love for Jesus.

We Catholics Believe

Lay missionaries are men and women who do not belong to religious communities. They work wherever people are poor and in need of the message of Jesus.

The **Works of Mercy** are actions performed by Christians to show their love and concern for others. There are Corporal works of Mercy (to help the body) and Spiritual Works of Mercy (to help the heart, soul, and mind).

Confirmation is one of the seven sacraments. Confirmation, along with Baptism and Eucharist, is a sacrament of initiation. These sacraments invite us to help Jesus in His saving work.

Development: We Believe

A New Commandment

Jesus and His friends ate many meals together. At the Last Supper, on the night before He died, Jesus got up from the table. He poured water into a large bowl and began to wash His friends' feet. Even though the servants were supposed to do this job, no one said anything.

Then Jesus came to Peter. "Surely, you're not going to wash my feet!" Peter exclaimed. "You are my Master and Teacher!"

"I know you don't understand what I am doing now," Jesus told him. "But someday you will understand."

"No," Peter said firmly. "You will never wash my feet. The servants can do it."

But Jesus replied, "Unless I wash you, you cannot share in My life."

Peter still did not understand, but he let Jesus wash his feet.

When Jesus finished, He returned to the table. "Do you realize what I have done for you?" He asked His friends. "You call me 'Master' and 'Teacher' because that is who I am. If I can wash your feet, then you must wash one another's feet. I have given you an example tonight. What I have done for you, you should do also. I give you a new commandment: Love one another, as I have loved you. When people see your great love for one another, they will know that you are My friends."

(based on John 13:5–15; 34–35)

Thinking about Scripture

- Why are love and service signs that Jesus is present?

APPLICATION: WE LIVE OUR FAITH

Showing Mercy

Match each work of mercy in Column A with its example in Column B.

A

_____ 1. Feed the hungry.
_____ 2. Give drink to the thirsty.
_____ 3. Clothe the naked.
_____ 4. Shelter the homeless.
_____ 5. Visit the sick.
_____ 6. Visit the imprisoned.
_____ 7. Bury the dead.

B

a. You make a get well card for a sick friend.
b. You help a little lost boy find his mom.
c. You pray for your Grandmother, who died.
d. You are nice to a girl everyone laughs at.
e. You help your little brother get dressed.
f. Your mother asks you to make some lemonade.
g. You share your favorite cookies.

Circle the **T** if the statement is true. Circle the **F** if the statement is false.

1. The only way you can help others is to die for them. T F

2. Helping others is a way to thank Jesus for His love. T F

3. Jesus said that it is all right to hit someone who has hit you first. T F

4. Helping others is something only adults can do. T F

5. The Holy Spirit helps the members of God's family work for peace and justice. T F

Vocabulary

In your own words, tell what these mean:

Works of Mercy _____

Jesus' new commandment _____

APPLICATION: WE PRAY

The Eucharist in Action

Leader: We gather as a family in the name of the Father, and of the Son, and of the Holy Spirit.
All: Amen.
Leader: Jesus teaches us a way of thinking and acting that is called the Beatitudes. Beatitude means "blessed" or "happy." If we live this way, we will be happy forever. Let us pray. Blessed are the poor in spirit.
All: They trust in God and put God first in their lives.
Leader: Blessed are they who mourn.
All: They are promised comfort and compassion.
Leader: Blessed are the meek.
All: God knows how great they are.
Leader: Blessed are those who hunger and thirst for what is right.
All: They treat others with respect and fairness.
Leader: Blessed are the merciful.
All: They are willing to forgiven and forget.
Leader: Blessed are the pure of heart.
All: They show us God's goodness and love.
Leader: Blessed are the peacemakers.
All: They make our world a better place.
Leader: Blessed are they who are persecuted for what is right.
All: They remind us to never give up.
Leader: Let us pray together.
All: Dear Mary, we call you blessed, so your life must have been a happy one. You answered God's call to be the Mother of Jesus and our Mother, too. Help us to live the Beatitudes. Amen.

Family note: Lesson 8 covers the Concluding Rite of the Mass when we are sent to "go in peace to love and serve the Lord." You may wish to talk to your child about everyday ways to serve others as Jesus calls us to. The prayer service centers on the Beatitudes, specific ways to follow Jesus.

Glossary

Alleluia   A word that means "praise God." Catholics use Alleluia! as a special expression of joy in the Risen Christ. At Mass, the Alleluia is sung before the Gospel, and often used in hymns of joy. (*page 21*)

Altar   The table around which Catholics gather to celebrate the Eucharist. (*page 56*)

Amen   A word meaning "Yes, I agree with what has just been said." When Catholics say Amen at the end of a prayer, they are agreeing with what was said in the prayer. The Great Amen at Mass is the people's way of saying yes to all that was said during the Eucharistic Prayer. (*page 49*)

Apostle   A close friend and follower of Jesus. Jesus sent the Apostles to build the kingdom of God. (*page 40*)

Baptism   A sacrament of initiation. It gives new life, washes away sin, and joins us to the Christian community. (*page 9*)

Bishop   The leader of a diocese who serves the people by preaching and teaching. (*page 40*)

Blessed Trinity   Our name for the one God who is Father, Son, and Holy Spirit. (*page 9*)

Candles   Objects lit on the altar during Mass as a reminder that Jesus is the Light of the World. (*page 57*)

Catholic   A word that means "open to everyone." Members of the Catholic Church are baptized and follow the pope and the bishops. (*page 9*)

Chalice   The cup that contains the wine at Mass. (*page 56*)

Ciborium   The covered bowl or dish that holds the people's Communion Bread, or Hosts. (*page 56*)

Communion   A name for receiving Jesus Christ in the Eucharist. The word communion means "unity with." (*page 57*)

Confession   Telling one's sins to the priest in the sacrament of Reconciliation. Another name for the sacrament of Reconciliation. (*page 17*)

Confirmation   A sacrament of initiation. It completes the sacrament of Baptism by strengthening us in the Holy Spirit. (*page 65*)

Conscience   A gift from God that helps us choose between right and wrong. We form our conscience throughout our lives. (*page 17*)

Corporal   The word corporal means "body." The Body and Blood of Christ are placed on the corporal, or napkin, at Mass. (*page 56*)

Cruets   Small bottles that hold the water and wine used at Mass. (*page 56*)

Deacon   An ordained minister who serves the community by helping the bishops and priests. (*page 40*)

Disciples   People who freely choose to follow Jesus and to learn from Him. (*page 26*)

Glossary

Eucharist   A sacrament of initiation that celebrates Jesus' presence in Holy Communion. The word "Eucharist" means "thanksgiving." (*page 9*)

Fish   A secret sign used by the early Christians to help other Christians know who they were. The outline of the fish was used during the time when the Roman empire persecuted people for following Jesus. Christians used this sign because, in Greek, the first letters of the words "Jesus Christ, God's Son, Savior" spell the word fish. (*page 57*)

Forgiveness   The act of pardoning someone who has caused a hurt. (*page 16*)

Genuflect   To kneel on one knee as a sign of respect for Jesus, our King. (*page 49*)

Gospel   A word that means "good news." In the Bible, there are four Gospels: Matthew, Mark, Luke, and John. Each Gospel tells about who Jesus is, what He did, and what He taught. (*page 24*)

Grace   God's life and love within us. (*page 9*)

Great Amen   At Mass, when the people say yes to what was said during the Eucharistic Prayer. (*page 49*)

Holy Days   Special days when Catholics show their membership in God's family by attending Mass. The Catholic Church in the United States celebrates six holy days: The Solemnity of Mary, Mother of God (January 1), Ascension Thursday (forty days after Easter), The Assumption of Mary (August 15), All Saints' Day (November 1), The Immaculate Conception of Mary (December 8), and Christmas (December 25). (*page 9*)

Hosanna   A word meaning "to shout with joy to the Lord." Catholics say Hosanna during Mass because they remember that Jesus is the Savior, and they give thanks for His love. (*page 41*)

Host   The Communion Bread. (*page 56*)

Last Supper   The special meal Jesus shared with His disciples on the night before He died. At the Last Supper, Jesus changed bread and wine into His own Body and Blood. He told His disciples to "Do this in memory of Me." (*page 41*)

Lay missionaries   Men and women who do not belong to religious communities. They work wherever people are poor and in need of the message of Jesus. (*page 65*)

Liturgy   A word that means the "work of the people." In liturgy we use more than words to pray. We also pray with our bodies, by the gestures and actions we use. (*page 49*)

Martyr   A follower of Jesus who dies because of his or her faith. The word means "witness." (*page 40*)

Ministry   Loving service to others. In Baptism, every Christian is called to the ministry of service. (*page 33*)

Glossary

Miracle A sign of God's power and love at work in the world. The miracles of Jesus show God's power to heal, to forgive, to nourish, and to set us free. (*page 25*)

Pall A stiff, cloth-covered card which the priest places over the chalice. The pall keeps anything from falling into the chalice. (*page 56*)

Parable A special story used by Jesus to teach His Way. Jesus told these stories using everyday things that were familiar to the people of His day so that they would understand the story's message. (*page 25*)

Parish A community of Catholics who gather to worship together and to help others. A parish is usually led by a pastor and is served by many parish ministers. (*page 33*)

Passover The Jewish feast of the Unleavened Bread that remembers the time God led the Israelites out of slavery to freedom. Jewish people celebrate this feast every spring with a special meal called "Seder." (*page 41*)

Paten The plate used for the bread at Mass. (*page 56*)

Penance An action that shows sorrow for sin. We receive penance as part of the sacrament of Reconciliation, to help us practice following Jesus better. Catholics also do penance at special times of the year, such as during Lent. Another name for the sacrament of Reconciliation. (*page 17*)

Penitential An attitude of sorrow for sin. People who are penitential take responsibility for their wrong choices and actions. They seriously try to change for the better. (*page 17*)

Prayer Any act of showing your love for God. Speaking and listening to God. The four types of prayer are praise, thanksgiving, petition, and sorrow for sin. (*page 48*)

Reconciliation The sacrament that celebrates God's forgiveness. In this sacrament, a person confesses his or her sins to a priest. The person expresses sorrow for these sins and promises to do better in the future. The priest forgives the person, in the name of God and the members of God's Family. (*page 17*)

Sacrament Signs and celebrations of God's power and love. The seven sacraments celebrated by Catholics are: Baptism, Confirmation, Eucharist, Reconciliation, Anointing of the Sick, Marriage, and Holy Orders. These sacraments give God's own life, or grace, to the members of the Church. They help the members to grow. (*page 9*)

Sacrifice Something precious offered to God out of love and worship. (*page 33*)

Savior A word that means "one who saves." Savior is another name for Jesus. (*page 41*)

Glossary

Sin Turning away from God and the community. Venial sin is choosing something that is wrong. Mortal sin is choosing something that is very seriously wrong. When we are truly sorry, we receive absolution for sin in the sacrament of Reconciliation. (*page 17*)

Tabernacle The place where the Eucharist is kept in the church at all times. (*page 56*)

Temptation The pull we all feel toward doing what we know is wrong. Jesus showed us how to say no to temptation. (*page 17*)

Unleavened bread Bread that contains no yeast. When the Israelites left Egypt, they could not wait for bread to rise. So, they ate only unleavened bread. Today, the Eucharistic Bread at Mass is unleavened bread. (*page 41*)

Vestments The special clothing worn by the priest and other ministers at Mass. The vestments often have signs of our faith on them. (*page 57*)

Word of God God's message, told to us by Jesus. This is also a name for Scripture because we believe God speaks to us in the Bible. (*page 24*)

Works of Mercy Actions performed by Christians to show their love and concern for others. Corporal Works of Mercy help meet the physical, or bodily needs of others. Spiritual Works of Mercy help meet their spiritual needs. (*page 65*)